IF THE WORLD...

Gyles Brandreth

Illustrated by Paul Dowling

BEAVER BOOKS

A Beaver Book
Published by Arrow Books Limited
62–5 Chandos Place, London WC2N 4NW

An imprint of Century Hutchinson Ltd

London Melbourne Sydney Auckland
Johannesburg and agencies throughout the world

First published 1989

Text © Victorama Ltd 1989
Illustrations © Paul Dowling 1989

Set in Century Schoolbook
by JH Graphics Ltd, Reading

Printed and bound in Great Britain by
Anchor Press Ltd, Tiptree, Essex

ISBN 0 09 960710 7

CONTENTS

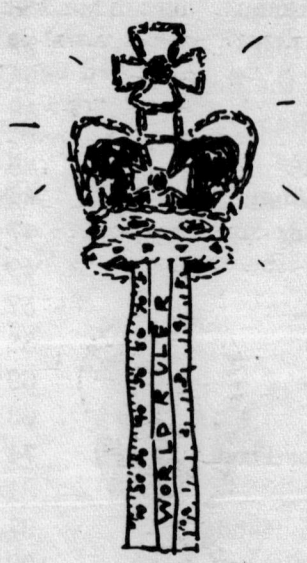

Introduction

If you've ever looked around your family, or your school, or your town, or even at international events in the news, and thought to yourself, if I ruled the world, things would be different, here's your chance to prove it. This book is your opportunity to decide the way the world should be run. You can change your home, your parents, your friends, your teachers; you can ban lessons and the food you hate, design your personal palace, decide what's on TV every night and award everyone extra pocket money − if *you* want to.

You hate Nick Astley, cabbage and your next-door neighbours? Then ban them. You love cream eggs and *EastEnders*? Pass a law so that you can have them every day. You'd like to rule the world from the top of the Empire State Building? That

can be arranged, no problem — and so can a Rolls-Royce, a helicopter, and whatever else your heart desires. While you're at it, find out how other rulers around the world have run things, and have a go at solving some of the major issues of today, including the problems of poverty, war, pollution and crime.

Writing this book has been easy — I've just asked the questions. Now it's up to you to provide the answers. I hope you'll have lots of fun thinking up brilliant new ideas to make the world a better place for everyone to live. And remember, you may be young, but your ideas and opinions are just as important and interesting as anyone else's. If someone tells you that you're too young to rule the world, remind them of King Henry VI, who came to the English throne in 1422 at the age of only nine months!

Gyles Brandreth

Titles First

Congratulations! You have just been made ruler of the world. As the most important person ever recorded in history, you're going to need a very impressive title. What do you fancy? Of course, your title may depend on the way you want to rule the world. If you're going to make all the decisions yourself and be in complete control, a title like King, or Emperor, or Shah, or Maharajah or Sultan would be suitable. Perhaps you could string a few of those titles together. How about 'His Majesty, Sultan Justin Brown, Supreme Ruler of the World'? It sounds very important, doesn't it?

If, on the other hand, you're not going to rule the world single-handed and would prefer to be the head of a world government, you might choose a title like Prime Minister, or President, or Governor. 'President Emma Jones, Leader of the World' has the right sort of ring about it. Personally I rather like the idea of 'His Ultimate

Cleverness, Emperor Gyles Brandreth I', but perhaps you would prefer something more simple like The Boss, or World Chief. And then again, you could make up a totally new title that no one has ever heard of before. Remember, as ruler of the world, you're in charge. What's your title going to be?

IF I RULED THE WORLD MY TITLE WOULD BE: _Maharajah Emperor Shah._

Short Cuts

It's all very well having a wonderfully grand title like 'Her Complete Perfection, Sultana Tracy Higgins, Mega-Leader of the Universe' – but it's not very practical, is it? Just imagine: every time someone wanted to ask what you'd like to eat for lunch it would take them two minutes to pronounce your title! What you need is a short title to make everyday life more easy. When she's not known as 'Her Majesty, Queen Elizabeth II', the Queen is addressed simply as 'Ma'am'. What would you like for your short title? It could be something plain and simple, like Sir or Miss, or it could be something completely new – a title that no one else is allowed to use.

IF I RULED THE WORLD MY SHORT TITLE
WOULD BE: _____Emp_____

_____

_____

Signing On

Throughout history, many rulers have used signs as symbols of their power and authority. These signs have taken many forms. British kings and queens have had coats of arms displaying wonderful beasts like lions and unicorns. The rulers of Ancient China chose the dragon as their symbol. Other rulers have designed their own flags. The leaders of the Russian Revolution in 1918 devised a flag showing a hammer and sickle on a red background. The hammer stood for those people who worked in industry in the towns, and the sickle for the people who worked in the fields, growing food. Red was the colour of revolution. Other flags have been strange shapes, like Nepal's, which is two triangles joined like the teeth of a saw, each with a face in the middle.

What would you like to appear on your own flag and coat of arms? There's no need to have lions and unicorns or hammers and sickles, just because everyone else has. If you like dogs or rabbits or squirrels you could have them supporting your coat of arms. And your flag can be any shape or colour you want, with whatever pictures you'd like on it. In the space below, draw your personal flag and coat of arms.

IF I RULED THE WORLD, I WOULD CHOOSE THIS FLAG:

IF I RULED THE WORLD, THIS WOULD BE MY COAT OF ARMS:

World HQ

Now you're in charge of the entire world you'll have to decide where you're going to rule it from. You could always try running it from your bedroom, but things might get a bit crowded. So perhaps it would be a good idea to set up a World HQ – and that could be whatever, and wherever, you like. It might be nice to have World HQ somewhere warm and sunny, like Spain or Australia. Or how about having it at the top of the world, at the North Pole? Too cold? It's up to you to choose where you'd like it to be. And while we're on the subject, what would your World HQ look like and what would you call it?

The emperors of China used to run their country from their palace in the Forbidden City in Peking. It was called the Forbidden City because if anyone went in without an invitation the penalty was death. Inside the walls of their incredible head-quarters the Chinese emperors had 800 buildings with 9000 rooms. There were magnificent palaces, streams and bridges, huge gardens, temples, theatres, libraries – even a tennis court, built for the very last emperor. At around the same time in Cambodia, now known as Kampuchea, the Khmer rulers built an amazing palace at Angkor. It had huge temples and lakes, but it had to be abandoned because the lakes attracted flies that bred malaria,

14

a deadly disease that could not be cured. And on a slightly smaller scale, Louis XIV of France built a palace at Versailles in the 1600s. Although its hundreds of rooms and wonderful fountains made it the most impressive palace in Europe, there was one problem — there wasn't a single loo in the whole place!

But *your* palace doesn't have to be anything like these old cities and buildings. Perhaps you could put it on board a huge ship which sails around the world and stops off to let you visit all your countries, or maybe it could be on board a giant airliner or even a spacecraft, circling the Earth. Use your imagination to devise something that even the emperors of China or Louis XIV would envy!

WORLD H.Q.

IF I RULED THE WORLD MY PALACE WOULD BE IN: USA- Florada

MY PALACE WOULD BE CALLED: Flourance

THE NUMBER OF ROOMS MY PALACE WOULD HAVE: 50

MY PALACE WOULD LOOK LIKE THIS:
(You can draw either a ground plan, looking down on your palace as if the roof had been lifted off, or a picture of how the outside would look.)

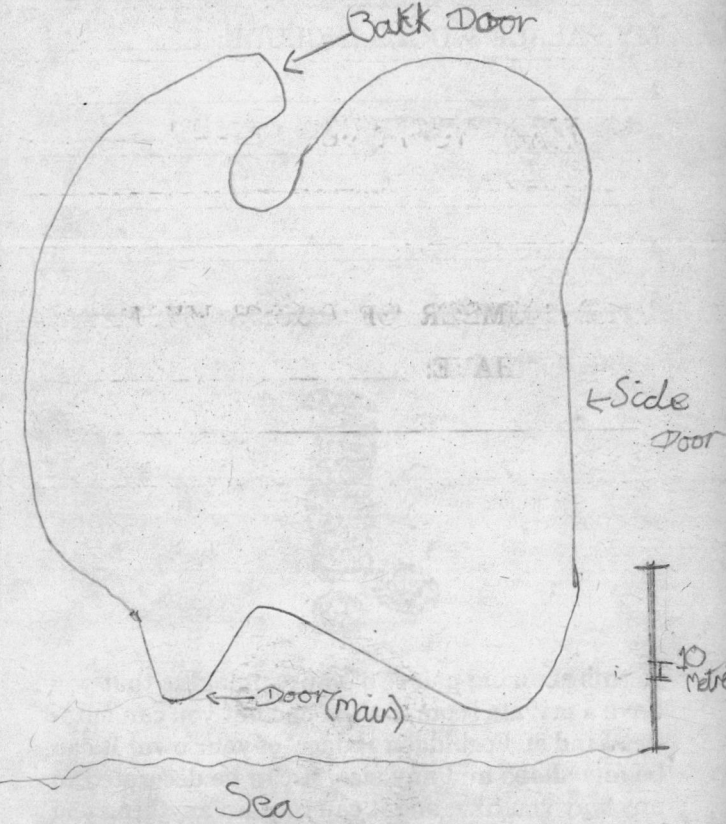

Back Door

Side Door

Door (main)

10 metre

Sea

As ruler of the world, your palace can be as luxurious or as weird as you'd like. Can you think of five things that your ideal home would have in it, or in the grounds? Mine would have a swimming pool with a huge waterchute to whizz down, a private funfair and a special garden for displaying my collection of garden gnomes — what about yours?

MY PALACE WOULD INCLUDE: _____

1 ___A Little Chei___

2 ___Extra Large Swimming P__

3 ___Funfain (with Rollacoanter)___

4 ___Air Port___

5 ___Chocolate Factoory___

In this amazing palace of yours, imagine that you have a private room that no one but you can enter — a kind of 'Forbidden Palace' of your own! It can be any shape and any size, it can be decorated in any way you like, and it can contain anything you want. Let your imagination run riot. The floors could be covered in carpet, or grass or wood. The walls can be whatever colour you choose. You can furnish it however you want. What will your room look like?

THE SHAPE AND SIZE OF MY ROOM WOULD BE:

(Draw a plan of your room here and show whether it is a big room or a small one. It doesn't have to be square or rectangular; it could be round or star-shaped!)

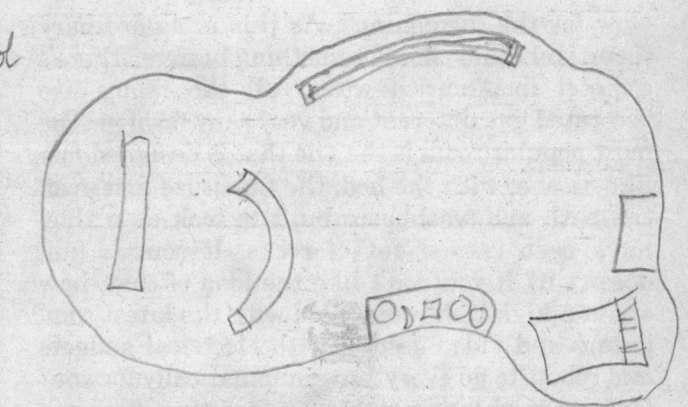

THE COLOUR OF THE WALLS WOULD BE:

White with green pound marks

THE FLOOR WOULD BE COVERED IN:
(Describe the colour if you're having a carpet.)

Red with gold around the egeg

Now for the furnishings. As this is no ordinary room, you could choose something bizarre. There's a hotel in America where all the rooms are decorated in a different and very zany fashion. The most popular room is the one that is designed just like a cave, with the bed, the furniture and even the bath and washbasin built to look as if they have been carved out of rocks. It sounds fun, doesn't it? If you don't like the idea of that, how about a high-tech room filled with the latest computers and video games, with electrical gadgets and robots to do everything automatically for you? Or a room where everything — furniture, floor and walls — is soft so that you can bounce around as if it were a giant trampoline? Or a room full of animals? What is the most wonderful room you can dream up?

MY PRIVATE ROOM WOULD BE: _____

_____

_____

MY PRIVATE ROOM WOULD LOOK LIKE THIS:

(Draw an impression of how you imagine the room would look.)

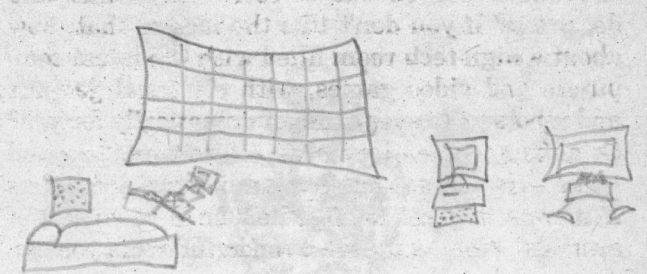

Good Advice

Ruling the world single-handed is an impossible task, so to help you you'll need some advisors. You could choose your friends, if they have the same kinds of ideas as you, or perhaps famous people who could give you the benefit of their advice. You might like Bob Geldof as one of your advisors, because he knows so much about the world

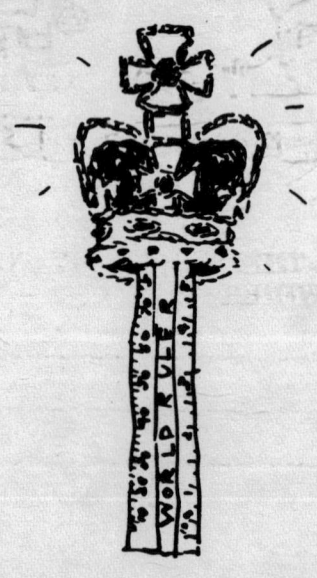

already, or the Queen, who has had plenty of experience, or maybe even your parents. Who are your advisors going to be?

The Ancient Chinese ruler Kubla Khan kept 5000 astrologers at his palace to act as his advisors. They consulted the stars and gave their predictions for everything he asked, from whether he would win a battle to what the weather would be like. It was a very tough job, because if they got their predictions wrong, he put them to death!

MY THREE ADVISORS

IF I RULED THE WORLD MY TOP THREE ADVISORS WOULD BE:

1 _Mum_

2 _Dad_

3 _Uncle Andrew_

Dressing the Part

You don't *have* to dress up to be a great leader. The Queen may wear a crown, but President Reagan and the Russian leader Mr Gorbachov don't wear a special uniform. However, many rulers feel that it's important to dress the part. In 1977 Jean-Bedel Bokassa crowned himself Emperor of one of the world's poorest countries, the Central African Empire. His crown, specially made for the occasion, cost nearly three million pounds, and his wife wore a dress covered in nearly three-quarters of a million pearls. The cost of the coronation came to nearly £17,000,000, which was a quarter of his country's annual income. When King George VI was crowned in Westminster Abbey in 1936, his velvet and ermine train was so heavy that at one point he got stuck and couldn't pull it!

You needn't go to these kind of extremes, but try designing yourself a special ceremonial outfit that will leave no one in any doubt that you are the most important person in the world. It doesn't have to be fashionable – it just has to make it clear to anyone who sees you that you're a very, very important person.

IF I RULED THE WORLD, MY SPECIAL OUTFIT WOULD LOOK LIKE THIS:

On the subject of clothes, are there any fashions you really dislike and would like to ban? I can remember about fifteen years ago when platform-soled shoes were in fashion. Not only did I look extremely silly in them, but I kept falling off and spraining my ankles! So I'd ban platform soles. What would you ban? Do you feel strongly about people wearing real fur coats or handbags made of crocodile skins? Perhaps you have other pet hates. Flared trousers? Mini-skirts? Leg-warmers? Fill in the space below.

IF I RULED THE WORLD THE CLOTHES I
WOULD BAN WOULD BE: _____

_____

_____

Do you think it would be a good idea if fashion were abolished throughout the world? The problem with fashion is that it changes so quickly we're always having to buy new clothes before our old ones have worn out. Just think of the waste of money.

There's another thing too, and that's the fact that we judge people by the outfits they wear. If someone wears very expensive clothes we often treat them better than someone who dresses scruffily. To do away with this inequality, some societies have abolished fashion. After the communist revolution in China in 1912 everyone wore a plain dark-coloured trouser suit. In fact the only clothes manufactured in the factories were plain trouser suits, because no one needed anything more fancy. Boring? Perhaps, but at least it solved the problem of what to wear every day!

Another fashion thought. Is it fair that in the rich western countries we should have so many different, impractical kinds of clothes, when elsewhere in the world people have hardly anything to wear? What would you do about fashion if you ruled the world?

WHAT I'D DO ABOUT FASHION: _____

_____

_____

If fashion were abolished and everyone wore the same clothes, what sort of outfit would you design for the world? What range of colours would the basic outfit come in? Draw your design below. Remember, the outfit doesn't need to be made from traditional fabrics like wool and cotton. It could be made of anything, and it could be any colour, or any pattern you like!

MY DESIGN FOR A BASIC WORLD OUTFIT:

THE RANGE OF COLOURS FOR THIS OUTFIT:
*(Either describe the colours, or, if you have
pencils or felt-tips of the correct colour, show an
example here.)*

_____

_____

_____

What additional items of clothing would you allow
everyone to have in their wardrobe? People who
lived in cold countries might need a heavy coat and
hat. What would you allow people who lived in
very hot climates to wear? See if you can think of
five extra items of clothing that everyone in the
world could have and list them here.

THE FIVE CLOTHING EXTRAS:

1 _____

2 _____

3 _____

4 _____

5 _____

Monumental Fame

The real test of fame and power is the kind of monument that is built to celebrate you. The Pharoahs of Ancient Egypt knew this, and they made sure that they would be remembered for thousands of years to come by creating some of the world's greatest monuments – the pyramids. Thousands of slaves were employed for years to build them, but all the hard work paid off. No one will ever forget the Pharoahs or their incredible power.

Another example of this kind of monument can be seen in China. In 1974 some peasants were digging a well when they came across life-sized pottery models of soldiers. Experts were called in, and when they began investigating the site they discovered more than 3000 of these soldiers, made out of terracotta clay. In another pit nearby they found 2000 more figures of charioteers, warriors, archers and spear-throwers. This incredible terracotta army is now on display in Xian, in China, and the archeologists are still digging – and still finding more soldiers! The figures were made for the tomb of China's first Emperor, Cheng, and buried in about 210BC.

Imagine that, as ruler of the world, you can design your own monument and decide what you'd

like to have named after you. What's the most
ambitious, incredible thing you can think of?

**IF I RULED THE WORLD MY MONUMENT
WOULD BE:**
(Describe your monument here.)

_____

_____

_____

(Draw in this space.)

My Honours List

In 1347 King Edward III decided to found an order of chivalry. He wanted to call it the order of St George and to honour his friends and advisors by making them Knights of the Order of St George. But before he could get his plan off the ground, something happened to change his mind. He was dancing at a ball when the garter which was holding up the stocking of one of the ladies, called Joan, the Fair Maid of Kent, fell to the floor. Everyone laughed and poor Joan was embarrassed. To save her blushes the King picked up the garter and fastened it around his own leg, saying *'Honi soit qui mal y pense'* – which, in translation from French, means 'Shame on him who thinks evil of it'. This was such a good saying that it became the motto of the new order of knights. And rather than call it the Order of St George, King Edward decided to call it the Order of the Garter.

That may sound like a pretty silly story but, six hundred years later, the Order of the Garter is still going strong. Each year, on a Monday in June, the Queen and the Knights of the Garter, wearing flowing blue capes and hats with feathers in them, attend a special service in St George's Chapel at Windsor Castle. It's a great privilege to join the Order, and the Queen honours only a few people by making them Knights of the Garter. There are many other ways in which she honours people, however. In the New Year Honours List and the Birthday Honours List, which are published each year, hundreds of people receive an official honour for their good deeds or long years of work. Some are made Lords; others are made Members of the British Empire and are allowed to put the letters MBE after their names.

As leader of the world, perhaps you'd like to establish an order of chivalry of your own, like Edward III. You could make it even sillier than the Order of the Garter. How about the Order of the Kettle, or the Compact Disc, or the Earmuffs! Or you could invent some medals to give people. I like the idea of the JWD Medal (Jolly Well Done)!

IF I RULED THE WORLD I WOULD HONOUR PEOPLE WITH: _____

_____

_____

And now can you think of the first five people who deserve such an honour? They could be your friends, or your family, or famous people you think have made the world a better place!

IF I RULED THE WORLD MY FIRST FIVE HONOURS WOULD GO TO:

1 _____

2 _____

3 _____

4 _____

5 _____

The Order of the Boot

Having honoured the people you like, how about giving the Order of the Boot to those you don't like? Can you think of five people who deserve it? Perhaps there's a teacher who is always nagging you, or someone who makes your life a misery. Maybe there's someone on the television or radio that you really can't stand? Go on then – give them the boot!

IF I RULED THE WORLD I WOULD GIVE THE ORDER OF THE BOOT TO:

1 _____

2 _____

3 _____

4 _____

5 _____

What would you do with the people who have received the Order of the Boot and all the other people you feel like banishing? Throughout history, various rulers have devised their own ways of getting rid of the people they didn't like. Some they locked in dank dungeons or sentenced to even worse fates. Others were banished to out-of-the-way places, or marooned on islands. What would you do to people who really annoyed you?

IF I RULED THE WORLD, I'D GET RID OF

PEOPLE I DIDN'T LIKE BY: _____

_____

_____

If you were going to banish someone, where would you banish them to? Can you think of somewhere suitable?

IF I RULED THE WORLD, I'D BANISH PEOPLE

TO: _____

_____

_____

What's in a Name?

As ruler of the world, people will want to name things after you. Just think of all the things that were named after Queen Victoria: Victoria Station in London, Lake Victoria in Africa, the state of Victoria in Australia, the city of Victoria in Canada, Victoria sponge cake, and any number of hospitals and public houses! And King Edward VII had a potato named after him; that's not very dignified, is it?

The Roman emperor Augustus didn't wait for other people to name things after him. He did it himself, scrapping one of the old months of the year and renaming it August in his own honour.

Alexander the Great, who was a famous Greek leader, was also a bit of a big-head. Whenever he conquered a country he would name at least one of its towns after himself. That explains why there are so many places called Alexandria!

Can you think of something that you would like to be named after you? What about a day of the week? We could scrap Mondays and replace them with Gylesdays! Or a cake, like Queen Victoria. I wouldn't mind a Brandreth gateau – a rich chocolate cake oozing with cream, fudge and vanilla-flavoured icing. Mmmmm! Or how about a planet or a river? It's up to you. Using the space

below, fill in the thing you would like named after
you and describe what it would look like.

IF I RULED THE WORLD AND COULD
CHOOSE SOMETHING TO BE NAMED AFTER
ME, I WOULD LIKE IT TO BE: _____
_____
_____

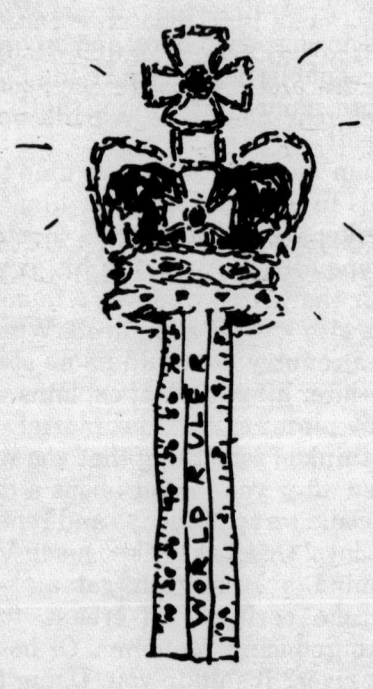

Money Galore

Now that you're in charge of the world, you can do what you like with all the money that is in circulation. Coins of one sort or another have been in circulation since the 7th century BC, and the first thing that most British monarchs and other leaders have done is to have new coins minted, with their faces on them. A similar design is used for bank notes and stamps. In the space below, draw one of your new coins, a bank note and a stamp showing your face.

IF I RULED THE WORLD, MY COINS, BANK NOTES AND STAMPS WOULD LOOK LIKE THIS:

On the subject of money, don't you think that with your new power as world leader it would be fun to scrap all the different currencies in the world and replace them with a single new one? Just think of all the problems it would solve. No one would have to change money when they went abroad for a holiday, and it would put an end to all the boring news about the rise of the dollar and the fall of the pound. What would you call this new currency and what would you name the different denominations? Wouldn't it be funny if we all bought things in potties, with one hundred pips to the potty!

IF I RULED THE WORLD, MY GLOBAL CURRENCY WOULD BE CALLED: _____

_____

_____

According to a survey published in a magazine called *Fortune* in 1987, the Queen is the richest woman in the world with property and savings valued at an incredible £5000 million. But the British royal family hasn't always been so rich. Some of them wasted so much money on fancy houses and palaces, like Buckingham Palace, that they nearly went bankrupt.

Naturally, being ruler of the entire world you have even more money to spend than the Queen. So what are you going to spend it on? Have fun filling in the top ten items on your shopping list!

IF I RULED THE WORLD, THE TOP TEN ITEMS ON MY SHOPPING LIST WOULD BE:

1 _____

2 _____

3 _____

4 _____

5 _____

6 _____

7 _____

8 _____

9 _____

10 _____

Having lots of money means that you can buy presents for people. Can you think of five people for whom you would most like to buy a present?

THE FIVE PEOPLE TO WHOM I WOULD GIVE A PRESENT:

1 _____

2 _____

3 _____

4 _____

5 _____

What would be the ideal gift for each of them? Remember, money is no object. What would they love to receive from you? It needn't be anything grand like diamonds, or a fur coat, or a Rolls-Royce.

Perhaps the best gift for a busy mother who hates the housework would be someone to do all the cleaning and washing for her. Or, for your little brother, someone to do his school homework for him!

IF I RULED THE WORLD, I'D GIVE THESE GIFTS:

1 _____

2 _____

3 _____

4 _____

5 _____

Mind Your Language

Don't you think the world would be an easier place to live in if we all spoke the same language? There are thousands of different languages and dialects spoken throughout the globe, so it's no wonder we have such difficulties communicating with each other. If you were going to choose a language which everyone in the world would learn, which would you choose? Chinese is spoken by more people than any other language, and English has already been selected as the language of diplomacy. Or perhaps it would be a good idea for us to speak a classical language like Latin or Greek?

IF I RULED THE WORLD, THE LANGUAGE I

WOULD CHOOSE WOULD BE: _____

_____

_____

Many other people have tried to find a solution to the problem of a global language. One of them was Dr L. L. Zamenhof, a Polish word expert who thought he had solved the problem by inventing Esperanto, a totally new language. He first introduced it to the world in 1887, and thousands of people took it seriously and began to learn to speak it. Esperanto is still spoken by eight million people around the world today and is a language accepted by the Post Office — so if you address a letter in Esperanto, it will get to its destination. If you were going to invent a totally new language, what would you call it?

IF I RULED THE WORLD I WOULD INVENT A

NEW LANGUAGE CALLED: _____

_____

_____

What kind of words would your new language include? In the list below are six words in English, and their translations in Esperanto. Try inventing words for your new language!

English	Esperanto
hot	varma
cold	malvarma
dog	hundo
house	domo
car	auto
daffodil	asfodello

Helping Hands

Throughout history, most rulers have had ordinary servants who have carried out all their everyday work for them, and they have also had servants whose job was simply to make life that little bit easier or more interesting. In aristocratic British households a few hundred years ago there was often a fool or jester, whose sole job it was to tell jokes, sing songs and cheer people up when they felt sad or bored.

Emperor Haile Selassie, ruler of Ethiopia until 1974, had rather short legs. When he sat down his feet would often dangle a few centimetres above the floor, which didn't look very impressive, particularly when he was sitting on his throne. So he employed a servant to go everywhere with him and carry a selection of cushions of varying thicknesses. The moment the Emperor sat down, this servant would pop the correct cushion under his feet, so that there was no embarrassing gap!

Even today, people still have servants to perform these little luxuries. The Queen Mother, for example, employs a bagpiper to play outside her window each morning as she has breakfast. It doesn't matter where she is — in London or on tour abroad — wherever she goes, so does her piper!

Is there one little luxury in your life that you'd like to have a servant to perform? I think I'd like to have a servant just to scratch my back when I get an itch that I can't reach myself! How about you?

IF I RULED THE WORLD I WOULD HAVE A

SERVANT TO: _____

_____

_____

Family Ties

A FAMILY TIE

The world is a very big and complicated place to run, so to begin with let's make some changes to something we all know about – families. All over the world, almost everyone grows up living in a family, usually with their mother, father, sisters and brothers. But before you start to imagine what your family would be like if *you* were in charge stop for a minute to think about families in general. There's no reason why children have to live with their families, is there? Once past the baby stage, they could all go away to live together in special children's communities. They'd never get lonely because there would always be someone to play with. And their parents wouldn't be around to nag and complain! Do you think it would be a

good idea to change the way that most of us grow up in families?

This sort of experiment, taking children away from their families, has happened many times in history. An everyday example is the practice of sending children to boarding school. But a far more extreme instance happened in Kampuchea when the leader Pol Pot took over the country in 1976. He decided to rid his country of all modern western influences and return to a medieval society. Everyone had to leave the towns and go to work in the fields. Machines were smashed. More than a million people died. Children were taken away from their parents and brought up together, under the guidance of Pol Pot's followers, so that they would grow up to become supporters of the new regime. Put like this, perhaps the idea of taking children away from their families doesn't sound so attractive.

There are lots of other issues that affect families. For example, what would you do about families where parents and children don't get on? If you couldn't live with your family for one reason or another, how would you like to live? What are your feelings about families? Are they important or not?

Would you like to leave your family? If you ruled the world, would you abolish families, as Pol Pot tried to, or preserve them? In the section below you'll find some of these questions. Try filling in your ideas!

MY IDEAS ABOUT FAMILIES:
Do you think families are important? If so, why?

_____

_____

Should children be allowed to leave their families
if they want? _____

_____

_____

How should children who don't have families be
looked after? _____

_____

_____

Can you think of anything you can do to make
family life better? _____

_____

_____

Now let's go from families in general to families in particular — your family. What do you like most about living with your family? Can you think of five things that you really enjoy about your parents and brothers and sisters?

THE THINGS I LIKE MOST ABOUT MY FAMILY:

1 _____

2 _____

3 _____

4 _____

5 _____

Are there things about living with your family that you really don't like? Perhaps you hate the kind of music that your father likes to listen to, or maybe you feel that your brother or sister gets more attention than you do. What five things about family life really drive you mad?

53

THE THINGS ABOUT MY FAMILY THAT DRIVE ME MAD:

1 _____

2 _____

3 _____

4 _____

5 _____

_____

Horrible Habit →

Everyone has bad habits — even me! (And being big-headed is one of my worst points.) Some people smoke, which is a pretty serious fault. Some people eat their peas with their knives. Others don't bother to pull out the plug when they've had a bath. What are the very worst habits of each member of your family?

MY FAMILY'S BAD HABITS:

_____

_____

_____

_____

You've revealed all the things you don't like about the members of your family, so now it's time to work out how to change them. You're in charge of your family now, so whatever you say goes. You could ban your father's old records from the house, or you could insist that he plays them in his own room — and he'd have to do it! If you could ban each member of your family from doing one thing that annoys you, what would you choose?

IF I RULED THE FAMILY, I'D BAN:

_____

_____

_____

_____

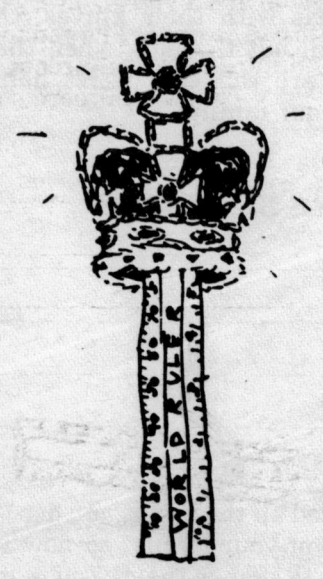

House Rules

Can you think of some rules that might make it easier for the members of your family to get on together? When I was young, my parents used to take decisions like where to go on holiday without consulting me, and they always got it wrong. What's more, they didn't like it if I complained! These days my first rule for happy family life is to have a discussion and a vote on every decision. My second rule is that no one is allowed to spend more than fifteen minutes in the bathroom. What rules would make your family run more smoothly.

MY FAMILY RULES: _____

_____

_____

Home Work

Most of us have to do some kind of work around the house, even if it's just making our own beds. Some chores, like dusting and tidying up, are really boring, but others are fun. I always like chopping vegetables because it gives me the chance to cut them into fancy shapes. Which household chores do you love, and which would you ban?

THE CHORE I'D BAN: _____

_____

_____

THE CHORE I LIKE DOING: _____

_____

_____

Ideal Homes

What's your house like? Do you like living there, or would you prefer to move? Perhaps you could do with an extra room or two for all the family? Maybe you live in a flat, and would prefer to live in a house with a garden? If you had the choice, what sort of home would you live in? List all the rooms and the extras, like a garden, stables, garages and so on.

IF I RULED THE WORLD, MY IDEAL HOME

WOULD BE: _____

_____

_____

(Draw a picture of your ideal home in this space)

What sort of equipment would your ideal home have! Mine would have a giant television, the size of a wall, and a whirlpool bath, and a dark room for developing photographs, to name just three things. If you could choose, what five luxuries would your house have?

IF I RULED THE WORLD, MY FIVE HOME

LUXURIES WOULD BE:

1 _____

2 _____

3 _____

4 _____

5 _____

Where would your ideal home be? Perhaps you like the street you're living in now, but you're not keen on the neighbours. Or perhaps you like your town, but not the part of it you're living in. Or, maybe you'd like to move your ideal home to a different place altogether. If you could do that, where would you live?

IF I RULED THE WORLD, MY HOME WOULD

BE IN: _____

_____

_____

Can you think of a good name to call your house? Most people aren't very imaginative when they name their home. The Halifax Building Society recently carried out a survey to see what the most popular names for houses were. Number one was The Bungalow. Number two was The Cottage. Number three was Rose Cottage. Number four was The School House. And Number five was The White House. Not very imaginative, are they? See if you can come up with something much more exciting and individual.

IF I RULED THE WORLD, MY HOME WOULD

BE CALLED: _____

_____

_____

TV Times

Let's start this section of the book by finding out about you. How much television do you watch in an average week? Using last week as a guide, fill in the number of hours in the sections below, then add them up.

THE NUMBER OF HOURS I SPEND WATCHING TV EACH WEEK:

	morning	*afternoon*	*evening*
Monday			
Tuesday			
Wednesday			
Thursday			
Friday			
Saturday			
Sunday			
Total			

Now that you've added up the total, are you surprised at how much TV you watch? Can you work out what proportion of your day is spent in front of the box? For example, if you watch two hours of television every day, that is one twelfth of your day. Three hours are equal to one eighth. How much of your life is spent watching TV?

THE PROPORTION OF MY LIFE SPENT

WATCHING TELEVISION: _____

_____

_____

Do your parents have strict rules about how much television you are allowed to watch? How long are you allowed?

THE NUMBER OF HOURS EACH WEEK I AM

ALLOWED TO WATCH TV: _____

_____

_____

Given the chance to watch all the TV you wanted, how many hours each day would you spend watching the screen?

THE NUMBER OF HOURS OF TELEVISION I'D

LIKE TO WATCH EVERY DAY: _____

_____

_____

As ruler of the world, wouldn't it be fun to choose what everyone sees on their TV screens! What top ten television programmes would you like to see on TV every day? You don't have to choose programmes that are on at the moment; you could choose your favourites from the past, like the *Tube* or *The Young Ones* or the first series of *Grange Hill*.

IF I RULED THE WORLD, THE TV PROGRAMMES I'D WATCH EVERY DAY WOULD BE:

1 _____

2 _____

3 _____

4 _____

5 _____

6 _____

7 _____

8 _____

9 _____

10 _____

Now here's a chance for you to create your personal TV hit list. Maybe you can't bear *Thomas the Tank Engine* or *Gardeners' World* – or is there something even worse? Here's your chance to ban them.

THE TV PROGRAMMES I'D BAN IF I RULED THE WORLD:

1 _____

2 _____

3 _____

4 _____

5 _____

Are there any TV presenters you can't stand? Can you imagine what life would be like without Terry Wogan on TV? Give the boot to whoever you dislike most!

THE TV PRESENTER I'D BAN IF I RULED THE WORLD: _____

_____

_____

Can you think of any really crazy television programmes that you would like to see on television? I've always wondered what it would be like if the cast of *Dynasty* was suddenly transferred to live in *Coronation Street*! What's the craziest TV programme you can think of?

THE CRAZY TV PROGRAMME I'D INVENT:

_____

_____

_____

Now for the news. Forget Sir Alistair Burnett — who would you *really* like to see reading the news? Roland Rat would be funny, but who would be your craziest TV newsreader?

MY CRAZY TV NEWSREADER: _____

_____

_____

Now let's look at TV from a different angle. Would you agree with the idea that time spent in front of the television is wasted time? Wouldn't it be better if you were out doing something useful rather than stuck in front of the box?

Watching some TV is all right but why should fit, healthy people sit around on the sofa watching for hours every day? Just think of all the work people could be doing if they weren't watching TV. Or they could be out playing sport and keeping fit, or picking up litter in the street, or just talking to each other.

In some Scandinavian countries there have been attempts to limit the amount of television people watch by making one day each week a TV-free day. Do you think that is a good idea? If you ruled the world, perhaps you would ban television altogether, or maybe just broadcast for a couple of hours each day. Would you ration the amount of time young people could spend in front of their screens? Or would you allow everyone to watch until they went square-eyed? Fill in the sections below with your ideas.

MY TELEVISION POLICY IF I RULED THE WORLD:

Is TV a good or bad thing:_____

_____

_____

TV rationing – a good idea?_____

_____

_____

Would you abolish TV? If so, why? If not, why not?

_____

_____

_____

There are lots of other difficult questions concerning television. Many people are worried by the influence that television has on our lives. They believe that the violence we see on our screens is sometimes copied in real life. Most of the time, television is just harmless fun. But sometimes it can be shocking. For example, some people find things like wildlife programmes, where they have seen a lion kill its prey, very upsetting. Have you ever seen anything on television that has frightened or upset you?

THE MOST SHOCKING TV PROGRAMME I'VE SEEN: _____

_____

_____

Do you think this programme should have been

banned? If so, why? If not, why not?_____

_____

_____

Try this TV check. For just one evening this week, watch the television programmes you would normally watch, but keep a pencil and paper by your side and note down how many times you see a violent scene. It doesn't have to be a scene in which someone gets badly hurt — it could just be a scene where people threaten one another, or fight. How many incidents will you see in one evening?

TV CHECK – THE NUMBER OF VIOLENT

INCIDENTS ON TV IN ONE EVENING: _____

_____

_____

At the moment on British television, programmes shown before 9pm are supposed to be suitable for family viewing. After that time, parents are supposed to decide what their children can watch. Have you ever seen a TV programme that you felt you really shouldn't have seen?

THE TV PROGRAMME I SHOULDN'T HAVE

SEEN: _____

_____

_____

Have you ever had to miss a programme because it was broadcast too late at night for you to watch? Do you think that this system is unfair, or do you agree that there are some things that you shouldn't be allowed to see?

THE TV PROGRAMME I WASN'T ALLOWED

TO SEE: _____

_____

_____

What would you do about this problem if you were in charge? Are there any solutions to make sure that everyone can see what they want to see, but no one gets upset or frightened?

IF I RULED THE WORLD, I'D SOLVE TV

PROBLEMS BY: _____

_____

_____

Food, Glorious Food!

Is there any sort of food that you really hate eating? Even if your parents are wonderful cooks, they probably sometimes serve up things that you're not very keen on. And how about school dinners? My pet hates were liver and coleslaw. Yuck! Here's your chance to ban things you hate from the menu at home!

IF I RULED THE WORLD I'D BAN: _____

_____

_____

Now you've banned the food you hate, here's your chance to list the things you'd like to see on the menu every day.

IF I RULED THE WORLD THIS IS THE FOOD

I'D EAT EVERY DAY: _____

_____

_____

Wouldn't it be fun to put together a global meal with the best food from the world's five continents! I think I'd start with some lovely spaghetti from Italy (Europe), then have an American hamburger and an Indian (Asia) poppadum, and finish with some delicious Pavolva from Australia and a cup of good Kenyan (Africa) coffee. Can you think of your ideal global menu?

MY GLOBAL MEAL:
(Include ingredients from all the five continents of the world:)

Europe _____

Asia _____

Africa _____

America _____

Australasia _____

If you could choose your favourite meal, what would it be? You can have anything in the world you like, no matter how strange it might be, so let your taste buds run riot!

IF I RULED THE WORLD, MY FAVOURITE
MEAL WOULD BE: _____

_____

_____

Hold on a moment! Let's look at this seriously. Maybe you're a very healthy person and your favourite foods are things that are good for you. In that case, you can skip this section. But my guess is that near the top of your list of favourites are things like chips, ice-cream, chocolate, biscuits, sweets and crisps. They're delicious, but if you lived on them you'd get fat and spotty and you probably wouldn't feel very well.

The terrible truth is that many of the foods we like best are bad for our health, while liver and salad are actually rather good for us. In some poor countries, where they have little money for luxuries like cakes and ice-cream, they have a healthier diet than we do. Knowing this, what are you, as ruler of the world, going to do about it?

FAVOURITE SCHOOL DINNERS

LIVER AND COLESLAW WITH GRAVY

You may feel that if everyone in the world chooses to live on hamburgers and chips, so what? There's a problem, though. If people eat the wrong things and become ill, it will cost you a lot of money to look after them — unless you're going to be a very tough ruler and just let them die! And people who are unhealthy are also often unhappy. So if you want the world to be a happier place, you should start by making sure that people are healthy. This is a problem that many politicians are trying to sort out. One British politician, Edwina Currie, has already been in trouble for suggesting that people in the north of England are less healthy than those in the south because of the kind of food they like to eat.

77

What are you, as ruler of the world, going to do about it? Are you going to let people eat what they want? Are you going to ban chips and chocolate? Are you going to pass a law making everyone eat salad once a week? Perhaps everyone should have a small patch of garden where they can grow their own fresh vegetables? Perhaps healthy food like liver and salad should be given away free in the supermarkets? You've probably got better ideas of your own, so fill them in below.

IF I RULED THE WORLD, THIS IS WHAT I'D DO ABOUT FOOD: _____

_____

_____

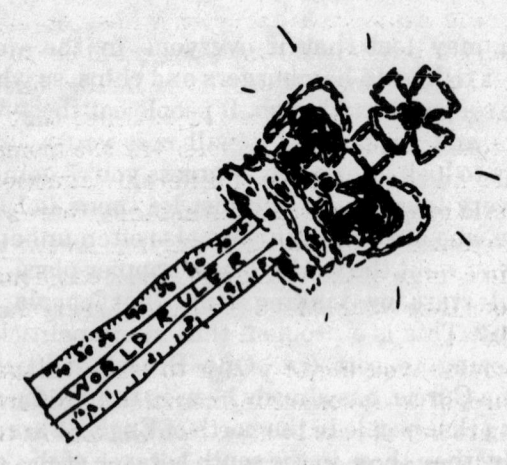

Here are some food facts. 2,000,000 pigs are turned into Spam each year. 1,200,200 chickens are killed every day in Great Britain for food. 10 acres of land (the area of five football pitches) planted with soya beans can feed 61 people for a year. 10 acres planted with wheat can feed 24 people for a year. 10 acres can support enough cows to feed two people a year. Each year millions of chickens spend their lives cooped up in tiny cages in which they can barely move. In factory farms, millions of pigs and calves are kept in small metal pens in barns and never see daylight.

Here's another fact. Around the world, millions of people live on the edge of starvation.

Sorry to be so serious, but ruling the world isn't just about palaces and dressing up and having fun. It's a big responsibility. You can change the world for better or for worse. For example, if countries like Britain stopped producing cows and sheep for meat, and grew soya beans or wheat or maize instead, the problem of starvation could be solved. So could the problem of cruelty to factory-farmed animals, though do you perhaps think that too much fuss is made about animals? At the moment, because all the hundreds of different countries of the world can't agree with one another, there's not much chance of anything changing. But if you were in charge of the whole world you could make decisions that would affect the lives of everyone on the planet.

Of course, you might prefer to leave things as they are, or to do something completely different. There are lots of possibilities. Bob Geldof has tried to help by sending seed, trucks and emergency food to Africa. Irrigation schemes have been developed as more long term solutions. Whatever your ideas on food, fill them in below.

IF I RULED THE WORLD, THIS IS WHAT I'D DO ABOUT:

Animal farming: _____

_____

_____

Eating meat: _____

_____

_____

The problem of world hunger: _____

_____

School's Out

Hooray for school! Well, at least it gives you somewhere to go on a cold, wet Monday morning. No matter how much you dislike going to school, there must be one lesson that's fun. Which, of all your school subjects, is your favourite?

MY FAVOURITE LESSON: _____

_____

_____

And which subject are you best at?

MY BEST SUBJECT: _____

_____

_____

Which lesson would you ban if you ruled the world? When I was a boy I used to hate sport so much that I'd do anything to avoid having to go out and play football or rugby. That was how I had my appendix

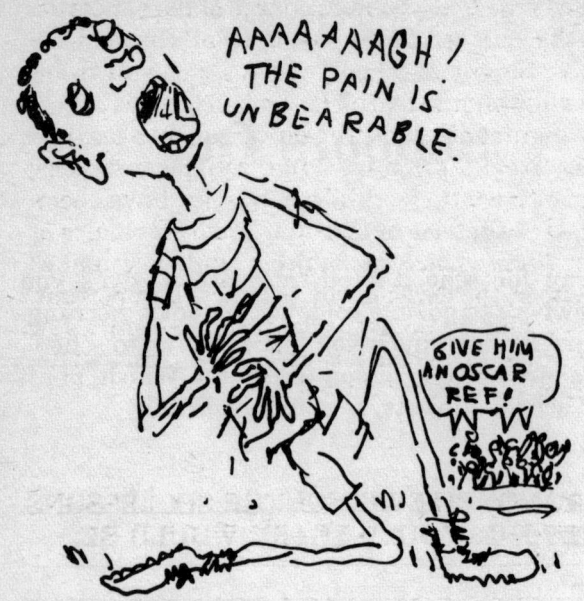

taken out. On one occasion before a games lesson I pretended my stomach was hurting – and before I had time to own up, I was taken to hospital. The doctor said I had appendicitis, and the next thing I knew I was off to the operating theatre! I didn't like to tell them it was all a hoax. If you hate sport, be careful about the excuses you make to get out of doing games!

IF I RULED THE WORLD, I'D BAN: _____

_____

_____

Imagine now that you're in charge of the education of all the children in the world. Of all the subjects that are taught in school, which six do you think every child should learn? If you had been at school in the eighteenth century you would have learned Latin, Greek, grammar and religious studies; eighteenth-century children would have been stunned at the idea of learning home economics or CDT! What choice of subjects will you make? Remember, the decision you take now is important. If you decide to do away with English, in a few years' time no one will be able to read and write. Think of the chaos that would cause!

IF I RULED THE WORLD, THE SIX LESSONS EVERYONE WOULD LEARN WOULD BE:

1 _____

2 _____

3 _____

4 _____

5 _____

6 _____

Now it's time to take a look at your teachers. Do you have a favourite teacher? Why do you like them? Perhaps because their lessons are very interesting and you learn a lot. Or perhaps because they're fair and don't pick on you. Or maybe even because they are very good-looking! Of all the teachers at your school, which do you like the best?

MY FAVOURITE TEACHER: _____

_____

_____

Because: _____

_____

_____

The worst teacher I ever had was called Mr Hatfield. We called him Hattie, and he used to throw pieces of chalk at anyone who didn't behave properly. He used to throw so much chalk, in fact, that one day he got into trouble with the Headmaster, who said he was wasting it! If you could ban one of your schoolteachers, which one would it be? And why?

IF I RULED THE WORLD, THE TEACHER I'D

BAN WOULD BE: _____

_____

_____

84

MY ~~FAVOURITE~~ WORST TEACHER IS MR. . . . . . .

HE SHOULD BE MARRIED TO MISS . . . . . .

85

I've often thought how much more interesting school would have been if we'd been taught by famous people. For example, biology would have been really great if David Bellamy had taught us. Think how much better it would be if you had a pop star to teach you music or a football star to teach sport! What 'famous' teachers would you like to have at your school?

IF I RULED THE WORLD, MY FAMOUS

TEACHERS WOULD BE: _____

_____

_____

Does your school have a uniform that you have to wear, or can everyone wear what they like? Do you think it's a good idea to have a uniform or not? Some peopple support the idea of having a school uniform because they say that it makes everyone look the same whether they're rich or poor, trendy or old-fashioned. On the other hand, school uniforms are sometimes hideous!

MY THOUGHTS ON SCHOOL UNIFORM: ____

_____

_____

If you were in charge of the world — and therefore the world's schools — would you abolish school uniforms, or would you design a uniform that every schoolchild in the world could wear?

IF I RULED THE WORLD, MY SCHOOL UNIFORM WOULD BE: _____

_____

_____

Here's your chance to design a school uniform to be worn all over the world. Use your imagination to design something practical and attractive that no one would mind wearing. You don't have to stick to the old-fashioned blazer and tie. What colours will your uniform be? Not navy blue, *please!*

MY GLOBAL SCHOOL UNIFORM:

Can you think of any really brilliant ideas that would make school more fun, teach you lots of new things and, with a bit of luck, make the world a better place to live in? I think that if I ruled the world, I'd pass a law so that every year each school in the world took its pupils abroad for a term. A school in Scotland could arrange an exchange with a school in Canada. A school in France could swap with a school in Thailand. That way all children would get an idea of what it's like to live in other parts of the world. They'd certainly learn a lot! What would your amazing school law be?

MY AMAZING SCHOOL LAW WOULD BE: __

_____

_____

Did you know that in many Japanese schools, the pupils have to clean the classrooms and corridors and even cook lunch for everyone? Does that sound like a good idea to you? Cooking lunch for the school probably isn't much fun, but at least no one can complain about the food if they've cooked it themselves. And if pupils had to clear up the mess they make (and sometimes the graffiti too!) they might be more neat and tidy in the future. Perhaps this idea sounds too much like hard work to you, but can you think of some jobs that pupils at your school could do?

MY JOB FOR PUPILS: _____

_____

_____

Have you ever behaved really badly at school? Don't be ashamed about admitting it – most people get into trouble every now and then. Can you remember what happened when you were caught? Teachers have lots of strange ways of punishing pupils who misbehave. I had one who used to make us stand against a wall, then slide down it until we were in a crouching position with our backs flat against the wall. He'd make us stay there for five minutes, or sometimes even ten. You try it – it's agony!

Can you think of some suitable punishments for people who misbehave at school? If you've ever been in a class with someone who is always making trouble, you'll know how difficult it is to stop them fooling around. What should you do? Throw chalk at them? Put them outside the door? Make them run round the football pitch three times? Expel them? Try to think up a number of examples of bad behaviour and suitable punishments.

MY SCHOOL DISCIPLINE RULES:

1 Example: _____

Punishment: _____

2 Example: _____

Punishment: _____

3 Example: _____

Punishment: _____

Have you ever thought of changing the school day? In France, children start school at about 8am, have a short break for a snack at about 11am, and finish school at 1pm in time to go home for lunch. Their afternoons are free for sport, homework and enjoying themselves. Does this sound like a good idea to you? Or perhaps you'd prefer a lie-in in the mornings or a three-hour lunchbreak? Work out your ideal school day and fill in the details here.

THE SCHOOL DAY: _____

_____

_____

How about changing the school week? If Sundays are boring, why not send children to school on Sundays and give them Friday off? Or have the school day stretch from 9am to 5.30pm for just four days a week? Can you think of any reasons why this wouldn't be a good idea?

THE SCHOOL WEEK: _____

_____

_____

Now please turn your attention to school holidays. At the moment most schoolchildren get about fifteen weeks' holiday each year. Do you think this is too much or too little? Is the summer holiday too long, or do you like a long break? Would it be better to have one week off school each month, or to divide the school year into four terms with a three-week holiday between each? In the section below you'll find the year divided up into months and simple blocks of four weeks. Using different colours, colour in the weeks you'd spend at school and the weeks you'd spend on holiday.

THE SCHOOL HOLIDAYS:

January

February

March

April

May

June

July

August

September

October

November

December

Total weeks on holiday: _____

All these questions have taken it for granted that you think it's a good idea for children to go to school. In Britain everyone from the age of five to sixteen has to have full-time education, but throughout the world millions of children don't have proper schooling. The countries which don't have compulsory eduction are often the poorer nations. The richer a country, the longer its children tend to spend at school. That's because educating children and young people is very expensive. In poorer countries a lot of children have to go out to work — they don't have time for school.

Do you think schools are necessary? If you ruled the world, would you make sure that every child had a good education? Or would you abolish schools altogether? Between what ages should children have to go to school? Or perhaps everyone should go to school but just learn practical things like science and computer studies? Write down your ideas about education in the section below and give your reasons for them. Can you predict what changes your decisions will make to the world?

IF I RULED THE WORLD, MY EDUCATION POLICY WOULD BE:

Education for all/ban on education: _____

_____

_____

Because: _____

_____

_____

Changes to education: _____

_____

_____

Because: _____

_____

_____

Age to start school: _____

Age to finish school: _____

The result of these changes: _____

_____

_____

If you had been alive two hundred years ago, there's a good chance that instead of reading this book, you'd be hard at work. You might have been digging coal in a mine, or working fourteen hours a day in a huge, noisy mill making cotton cloth. If you were very unlucky, you might have been forced to climb up the inside of chimneys to sweep the soot out.

Today, the situation is very different, but there are many millions of children in Britain and around the world who still have to work for their living. In India some children are employed making very expensive carpets. They tie each thread of the carpet by hand, and their little fingers mean that they can do intricate work that the adults' hands are too big for. Unfortunately they are not paid well, and they can go blind because of the strain on their eyes. In Mexico City some children live on rubbish dumps, searching through people's garbage for food and items which they can sell. Understandably, many of them die of disease. The saddest thing is that the money these children earn is often the only thing that saves their family from starving.

95

If you ruled the world, would you want to do something about this problem? Would you ban children under a certain age from working? Can you imagine what the consequences of this ban might be? Would you make employers pay children a proper rate for their work? If so, how much? What would be the effect of raising their wages? It's a terribly difficult problem, but perhaps you can think of a brilliant way to solve it!

IF I RULED THE WORLD, MY POLICY ON

CHILDREN AT WORK WOULD BE: _____

_____

_____

_____

_____

Time on
Your Hands

We all take it for granted that time is divided into days of twenty-four hours, with sixty minutes in each hour and sixty seconds to each minute, but have you ever wondered why this should be so? Days are the most natural units of time, because it takes a day for the earth to rotate, going from light to darkness and back to light again. But hours, minutes and seconds have been invented for convenience.

We've got used to thinking that a year must be 365 days long, but there's no reason why it should be so. In fact in many societies, years have been different lengths. On Bali, for example, there used to be a system of long and short years that worked very well.

Now you rule the world, you could change the way we think about time. You could simplify it, so that we have a ten-hour day instead of a twenty-four hour one. While you're at it, you could change the number of minutes in each hour and the number of seconds in each minute. And you could certainly change the number of days we have each year. Have a think about it, then fill in the sections below.

IF I RULED THE WORLD, I'D CHANGE TO:

Number of hours in a day: _____

Number of minutes in an hour: _____

Number of seconds in a minute: _____

Number of days in a year: _____

See how your amazing system works by filling in the new and old times on the chart below. For example, if in a normal twenty-four hour day you usually get up at 8am, what time would you get up under your new time system? If you have chosen to have ten hours in your new day, and a hundred minutes in each hour, the equivalent of 8am would be around 3.30am. See if you can fill in all the spaces in the chart.

THE NEW DAY:

	Normal time	*New time*
Get up		
Go to school		
Lunchtime		
Finish school		
Dinner time		
Bedtime		

Now you've changed time, you'll have to redesign all the watches and clocks. What would your new clock face look like? In the circles below, draw the new-look clock and use the hands to show the times you have worked out in the chart above. For example, if you have worked out that according to your new time system you would have lunch at 5.20pm, show the hands in the right position.

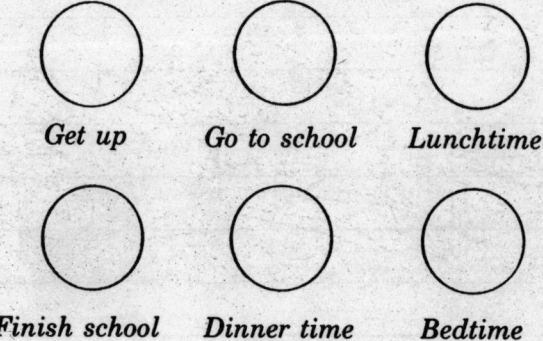

Get up   *Go to school*   *Lunchtime*

Finish school   *Dinner time*   *Bedtime*

Pop's the Question

I love music — any sort of music, from the latest top ten to schmaltzy old songs from musicals, and classical composers like Mozart and Beethoven. What are your musical tastes? On BBC Radio 4 there's a programme called *Desert Island Discs*, where famous people are told to imagine they've been cast away on a desert island. They're allowed to take their eight favourite records with them. Now that you rule the world, you're bound to be invited to go on the programme. Which eight records will you choose?

MY DESERT ISLAND RECORDS:

1 _____

2 _____

3 _____

4 _____

5 _____

6 _____

7 _____

8 _____

And which record do you hate so much you'd have it banned?

IF I RULED THE WORLD, THE RECORD I'D

BAN WOULD BE: _____

_____

_____

Did you know that the Greek national anthem has 157 verses? It must take hours to sing it all the way through! As a celebration of your reign as world ruler, it would be fun for you to choose a song to be used as a global anthem wherever you went. What would you like? I know which song I'd choose. It would be 'Imagine' by John Lennon, which is all about the way the world could be if we just used our imaginations to change things. Maybe you'd like something a bit more catchy? It's up to you!

IF I RULED THE WORLD, MY GLOBAL

ANTHEM WOULD BE: _____

_____

_____

Do you listen to the radio much? Which radio station would you choose to broadcast all round the world, for everyone to listen to?

IF I RULED THE WORLD, MY GLOBAL RADIO

STATION WOULD BE: _____

_____

_____

Is there a radio station, or a radio presenter, whom you hate? Who would you ban, given the chance?

IF I RULED THE WORLD, MY RADIO BAN

WOULD BE: _____

_____

_____

In the days before records and Walkmans, many rulers had their own personal musicians, called minstrels, who accompanied them wherever they went so that they could have music whenever they wanted. If you could have your own modern-day minstrel to sing you a song when you felt depressed, who would it be? Michael Jackson? Wet Wet Wet? Madonna? Or maybe you'd like all the members of the London Symphony Orchestra?

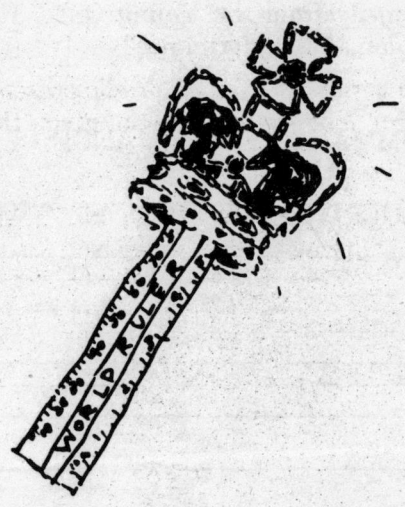

IF I RULED THE WORLD, MY MINSTREL

WOULD BE: _____

_____

_____

Each year the Queen goes to see the Royal Command Performance — a show of music, comedy, dance, magic and all kinds of fun. The Queen doesn't choose the acts herself, and it's rumoured that she finds some of the show boring. But imagine what it would be like if you could choose your favourite pop groups, comedians, TV stars and performers to put on a Command Performance for you! Try to think of ten acts you'd select for your perfect evening out. Mine would include music by the Beatles, songs from the Muppets, comedy from the Young Ones. How about your Command Performance?

MY COMMAND PERFORMANCE:

1 _____

2 _____

3 _____

4 _____

5 _____

6 _____

7 _____

8 _____

9 _____

10 _____

Kids' Lib

When I was young I spent a lot of my time thinking how unfair it was that there were so many things that kids weren't allowed to do. And it wasn't just that. Adults seemed to treat most children as if they were idiots!

I think that if I ruled the world, I'd write a Children's Charter which would aim to make life better for kids. It would have five rules. Here are my suggestions. See what you think of them, and add some of your own!

My first law would be about pocket money. One of the reasons children aren't taken very seriously in the adult world is that they don't have much money to spend. If every child in the world was given a set amount of pocket money each week, it would change the situation. There would be shops and banks and discos and restaurants for children, and kids could spend the money whichever way they wanted. Does this sound a good idea or not? How much money would you give to each child a week?

MY POCKET MONEY LAW: _____

_____

_____

If you had that amount of pocket money each week,

how would you spend it?_____

_____

_____

My second law would be about holidays. The kind
of thing that most adults like doing on holiday —
lying on beaches, walking round ruins or sitting
in the car in the rain — drive children crazy with
boredom. So I'd make it a law that once a year
every child went on an activity holiday and did
whatever he or she liked — from pony trekking and
learning to use computers, to windsurfing, drama,
pottery and BMX scrambling. Do you have a better
idea for making sure that kids get a good holiday
every year?

MY HOLIDAY LAW: _____

_____

_____

If you could go on a special activity holiday which

activities would you choose to do? _____

_____

_____

And now – sweets! Parents and children are always having rows about sweets. Children complain they're not allowed enough sweets, while parents say they have too many. If I ruled the world, I'd make sure each child got some sweets every Sunday, but not on other days. What law would you make about sweets? If you're going to allow sweets every day, what will you do about the problem of tooth decay? Perhaps you could pass another law making children brush their teeth twice a day!

MY SWEETS LAW: _____

_____

_____

What are your favourite sweets? Imagine that you have £5 to spend on them. What would you buy!

_____

_____

_____

My fourth law might sound rather silly, but I don't think it is. I think adults should be as polite to children as children are to adults. Do you agree? So I would make a law saying that if adults want

to go into a child's room, they should knock first and wait to be asked in before they barge through. Maybe you can think of other ways in which adults sometimes behave rudely towards children. What law would you pass to improve their behaviour?

MY POLITE BEHAVIOUR LAW: _____

_____

_____

My fifth law is about clothes. You may have parents who are very good at picking nice clothes for you to wear, but some parents are awful at it. Just when you're desperate for a red jacket and a pair of jeans, they go shopping and come home with a navy jacket two sizes too big and a pair of green woolly trousers – and then they make you wear them! If I ruled the world, I'd give every child a clothing allowance, which they could spend on the clothes they wanted. What do you think? Is there a better way of solving the clothes problem? If you like the idea of an allowance, how much would you give to each child?

MY CLOTHES LAW: _____

_____

_____

Late Night Laws

Something which drives a lot of young people mad is the time their parents expect them to come home each night. When I was at school, the latest I was allowed out was 8pm. If I went to a party, I usually had to come home before it had even begun! Do you have the same problem? If so, what time would you allow youngsters to stay out till?

IF I RULED THE WORLD, MY LATE-NIGHT

LAW WOULD BE: _____

_____

_____

If you ruled the world, would you stay up late every night? If the answer is yes, what kind of night-time adventures would have? Would you go dancing in a disco? Study the night sky with a telescope? Go to the pictures? Or do you have even better ideas for late-night fun?

MY LATE NIGHT FUN: _____

_____

_____

Age Ban

Do you like going to the cinema? If you do, you may have felt frustrated that you're not allowed to see some films that are shown because you're too young. Now that so many people have videos, it's not so much of a problem – but it's certainly annoying!

Do you think it's right that young people should be banned from watching certain films? Do you think it's right that there are some films that are banned altogether, so that no one can see them? These bans are imposed by a board of censors, who see all films and decide which are suitable for people to watch and which aren't. Do you think we should be allowed to watch what we want, or are there good reasons for preventing children and adults from watching certain films? Maybe you have little brothers and sisters. Do you think there are some things that they shouldn't be allowed to see? Think about it, then jot down your ideas and suggestions in the space below.

IF I RULED THE WORLD, MY POLICY ON

FILMS WOULD BE: _____

_____

_____

Town and Country

Do you like the town you live in? If you don't live in a town or city, think about the town nearest to you. Does it have all the facilities you'd like — like a cinema, a park, a theatre, an ice-skating rink, or a disco? If it has, that's wonderful. If it hasn't, can you think of five things that would make life in your town better?

IF I RULED THE WORLD, THE CHANGES I'D MAKE TO MY TOWN WOULD BE:

1 _____

2 _____

3 _____

4 _____

5 _____

Is there one place, or one building, in your town that you would like to change? It may be a horrible modern tower block that no one likes living in and which spoils the view. Or a hideous old building in the city centre. Or perhaps there's a derelict house that you don't like walking past on the way home from school?

IF I RULED THE WORLD, I'D KNOCK DOWN:

_____

_____

_____

Now, let's go from your town to towns in general. Which town or city do you think should be the capital of England, or Scotland, Wales or northern Ireland – or wherever you happen to live? London hasn't always been the capital of England. Winchester was once just as important. And north of the border, Stirling and Dunfermline have a history that rivals Edinburgh.

Perhaps you think this is a silly question to ask, but it's not. The capital city of a country is often in the most wealthy area because everyone flocks there. There are good roads and railways leading to it, and usually it has excellent facilities. Sometimes the rest of the country loses out because everything is centred around the capital. Some people feel this is happening in England, where the south-east area, around London, is much more affluent than the more outlying parts of the country, like the north-east and the south-west.

If you ruled the world, would you move the capital of your country to another city? In England, Manchester or Liverpool might be good places. Or do you think that London, or, if you change the other capitals in the UK, Edinburgh, Cardiff and Belfast have too much to lose? Perhaps you have ideas for a different solution to the problem. For hundreds of years, before London was accepted as the capital, the kings and queens of England had an answer. The capital was wherever they were – so it could move around every day!

IF I RULED THE WORLD, THE CAPITAL OF
MY COUNTRY WOULD BE: _____

_____

_____

Because: _____

_____

_____

Can you think of one thing you would change
about Britain (presuming you live in Britain!) to
make it a better place to live? I think I'd like to
change the climate so that it was warmer – but
what change would you make?

IF I RULED THE WORLD, MY BRITISH
CHANGE WOULD BE: _____

_____

_____

If you were given an allowance of, say £200 each year to spend on clothing, what would you buy? Would you blow it all on one posh outfit or buy lots of cheap things? Or would you buy something amazing, like an American football kit? The choice is yours. _____

_____

_____

If you had to write your own Children's Charter to make life easier for kids, what are the five things you would include? There's space below for you to create your own laws!

Law 1: _____

Law 2: _____

Law 3: _____

Law 4: _____

Law 5: _____

Problem Pets

Britain is supposed to be a nation of animal lovers, but did you know that more than a million dogs are put down every year? And that's quite apart from all the cases of cruelty and neglect that are reported. You may think that's bad, but in some countries the treatment of dogs and cats is much worse because they are not considered to be pets. The thought depresses me. If I ruled the world, I'd make some very strict rules about keeping animals so that only people who seriously wanted one, and were prepared to look after it, would have one.

First, I'd ban dogs from city centres and all parks. I like dogs, but they make a terrible mess. Then I'd introduce licences for dogs and cats. They wouldn't be cheap. I think I'd charge £100 a year for them. That way, people would have to take owning a pet very seriously and I hope they'd look after them better. With all the money raised by the licences, I'd start a pet warden service all over the country, and eventually all over the world, checking the licences and looking after strays. Does that sound too tough? Of course, there are drawbacks, for example there are a lot of elderly people living in cities who keep a dog or cat for a companion and couldn't afford the £100 licence fee. I haven't worked out what to do about them yet! Do you have other ideas about laws for pets? Write them down here.

IF I RULED THE WORLD, MY LAW ON PETS

WOULD BE: _____

_____

_____

In some parts of the United States dog-owners have to clean up after their animals with a pooper scooper. If they don't, they get fined. I think that's a great idea – do you? How much would you fine dirty dog-owners?

IF I RULED THE WORLD, MY LAW ON DIRTY

DOGS WOULD BE: _____

_____

_____

While we're thinking about pets, what are your opinions about the use of animals for medical experiments? Do you think we should make animals suffer in our search for cures for diseases? Would you ban animal experiments, or do you think they're justified because they might help humans?

IF I RULED THE WORLD, MY LAW ON

ANIMAL EXPERIMENTS WOULD BE: _____

_____

_____

Here's a silly question. If you ruled the world and could have any pet you liked, what kind of pet would you choose? It could be an ordinary pet, like a hamster or a puppy – or it could be something amazing, like a tiger cub or an elephant. Or it could be something quite out of this world, like a dinosaur, or a robot parrot, or a creature from space. What would you choose?

IF I RULED THE WORLD, MY PET WOULD

BE: _____

_____

_____

What would you call this special pet of yours? If your pet is a dog, please don't call it Ben. According to a survey done in 1986, Ben was the most common dog's name in Britain. Think what would happen if you went to your local park and yelled 'Ben!' Half the dogs in the neighbourhood would come running!

MY PET'S NAME WOULD BE: _____

_____

_____

(Now draw a picture of your pet in this space.)

Born to Shop

Everyone loves to go shopping, particularly when they've got plenty of money to spend. You can spend that money any day of the week in Britain – except Sunday, because most high-street shops aren't open on a Sunday. Do you think this is fair? In many countries around the world, particularly in America, you can shop every day of the week. In fact some shops are open twenty-four hours a day, just in case you need a new pair of shoes or some shampoo at 4am.

Christians argue that the Bible tells us that we should keep one day a week special, and not go out shopping. They are supported by many shop assistants, who say that it's bad enough having to work on a Saturday, let alone Sunday. Of course, in many countries there isn't much of an argument. In New Zealand, for example, almost all the shops still close at Saturday lunchtime! What's your opinion? Do you want to be able to buy a pair of shoes on Sunday, or are you keen to keep one day different from all the rest?

MY SHOPPING POLICY: _____

_____

_____

Traffic Trouble

I live in London, and I think one of the worst things about it is the traffic. There are so many traffic jams that it's often quicker to walk than go by car or bus, and the air is polluted by fumes from all the engines. In some places the exhaust fumes cause smog — a sort of thick, choking fog, which can be extremely dangerous. In Tokyo, Japan, some pedestrians wear masks to try to filter out the worst fumes, and recently the situation got so bad in Florence, in Italy, and Athens, capital of Greece, that the local authorities decided to do something about it. In Florence, cars are banned from the city centre completely. Far from complaining, most people like the peace and quiet and the chance to walk around without getting run over. In Athens, cars with even registration numbers are allowed in the city one day, and those with odd registration numbers the next day. It sounds a bit complicated, but it seems to be working.

If you ruled the world, would you ban traffic in the centre of your town? Would you ban traffic in the centre of *all* towns? Can you think of any other way of stopping traffic jams and pollution? Or do you just think that if the traffic jams get bad enough, people will stop using their cars anyway? Ideas here, please!

_____

_____

How about taking the argument banning traffic a bit further, and think about banning private vehicles altogether? Private cars use up millions of gallons of petrol each year and, one day, we'll use up the last of the earth's supplies. Private cars are also a terrible waste. Try this experiment. Go out into the street and count how many people are travelling in the first ten cars that go by. Most of them will probably have just the driver inside – no passengers in the other seats. What a waste!

And it's not just the waste of petrol that is causing problems. Petrol contains lead, and lead from car exhausts is poisoning some of the fruit and vegetables we eat. It may also be poisoning us directly, in the air.

When you look back over the span of history, we've only had cars for a very short time. In fact it's only during the last fifty years that ordinary people have been able to afford them. Before that, nearly everyone relied on public transport. Many experts would like us to go back to that time, and use more public transport, rather than go everywhere in our cars. What do you think? If the bus and train services were improved, would you use them more? If cars were banned in your town centre, would you go there by bus? Or do you think cars are the greatest things ever? Maybe there should be some sort of rationing, with just one car to a family? If you think there's a problem, have a go at solving it!

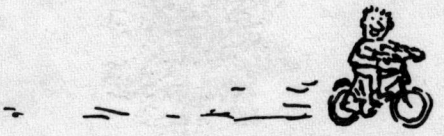

MY CAR POLICY: _____

_____

_____

It's always seemed very odd to me that we don't all drive on the same side of the road. It would make the world a much safer place. And what about road signs? Don't you think it would be easier if we scrapped all the national road signs and replaced them with a worldwide system?

If you ruled the world, which side of the road would you make people drive on?

MY DRIVING POLICY: _____

_____

_____

Now invent some new road signs to be used around the world. On the left are some current British road signs. Draw your new, improved versions on the right.

Road works

Hump bridge

Double bend

Slippery road

Road narrows
(on both sides)

Loose
chippings

On a fun note, if you ruled the world, what kind of car would you travel around in? I think I'd like two or three cars for different occasions. A Rolls-Royce for when I was feeling very grand, a sports car for fun, and a battered old family car. What about you?

IF I RULED THE WORLD, I'D DRIVE: _____

_____

_____

(Draw a picture of your car, or cars, here.)

Around the World

Have you ever been abroad? If you have, you'll have noticed that most countries have different sorts of customs and habits to those in Britain. Are there any customs you've encountered abroad which you would like to see introduced around the world?

When I go to France or Spain I enjoy the tradition of having a proper lunch hour, during which the offices and shops close and everyone goes home for a good meal and a nap, or siesta. Then at four o'clock everyone gets going again, refreshed for the evening. And although I've never been to the famous Carnival in Rio de Janeiro, Brazil, I've seen pictures of it, and it looks as if everyone has a marvellous time. So I'd make sure that there was a world carnival each year, with thousands of people and music and dancing, so that everyone could have a good time. What customs would you introduce if you could choose?

IF I RULED THE WORLD, MY GLOBAL

CUSTOMS WOULD BE: _____

_____

_____

Can you think of a new custom or festival you would like to invent? I think I'd invent the Cheer Up Festival, which would be the one day of the year when everyone could be silly and have fun. Everyone would have to tell someone else a joke. There'd be a special Cheer Up Day menu of peanuts, spaghetti and jelly, all of which you'd have to eat with chopsticks. And everyone would have to wear a silly hat or jumper. In the evening there would be fireworks and music.

And if you think that sounds too silly, consider all the festivals we already celebrate. There's Shrove Tuesday, for example, when people race each other – tossing pancakes in the air! Or St David's Day, when people pin leeks to their lapels! See if you can come up with anything sillier.

IF I RULED THE WORLD, MY NEW FESTIVAL

WOULD BE: _____

_____

_____

Which custom or festival would you abolish?
You're going to hate me for saying this, but I think
I might abolish Christmas. Not the religious side
of Christmas, but the commercial part of it — all
the expensive presents and food, and the hours
spent sitting in front of the television. There's
another custom I don't like very much, and that's
Morris Dancing, with all those men waving
handkerchiefs about and jangling the bells tied
round their knees. I think I might abolish that, too.
Maybe you've nothing against Christmas and
Morris Dancing — but what *would* you like to ban?

IF I RULED THE WORLD, I'D BAN: _____

_____

_____

World Matters

It's always seemed strange to me that all the other planets in the solar system have exotic names based on ancient Greek and Roman gods – like Neptune, Pluto, Venus and Mars – and our planet is called plain, ordinary earth. So if I ruled the world, I'd think of a new name for it. I'm not sure what. Perhaps Zeus, or Apollo in tradition with the other planets named after gods. Or perhaps something more like the kind of planets in *Dr Who* or *Star Trek* – Xercon, or Silmar, or Flyjoos. Would you re-christen earth? And if so, what would you call it?

What would you do about all the different countries that make up the world? Would you keep them as they are, or would you just scrap all the old national boundaries and make the world one big place?

The problem with having lots of small countries is that they all seem to try to do the best for themselves, but not for the world at large — if you see what I mean. And if two countries disagree about something, they sometimes have a war, which is not good for anyone and could, if nuclear bombs were dropped, kill us all.

If we belonged to one world and stopped thinking of ourselves as British, or American, or Belgian, or Kenyan, do you think that would help to solve some of our problems? Do you think we could do it? After all, most of us have a very strong sense of national identity. We feel proud to be British, or Australian, or Russian, so perhaps we wouldn't want to give it up. Do you have an answer to the whole problem?

IF I RULED THE WORLD, I'D: _____

_____

_____

Time for a quick quiz. What countries do these things symbolise?

> a shamrock
> an eagle
> a kangaroo
> a bear

The answers are the Republic of Ireland, the USA, Australia and Russia. It would be fun to think up a symbol for the whole world, wouldn't it? Your symbol doesn't have to be an animal or a plant. It could be a visual symbol – a picture that summed up your view of the world. That's my world symbol below. What would yours be? Draw it in the space provided.

IF I RULED THE WORLD MY WORLD SYMBOL WOULD BE:

Tough Problems

This section of the book is all about the really tough problems that rulers have had to face. Some of these problems have flummoxed politicians, kings and law-makers for years, and they've left the world in a terrible mess. See if you can come up with something better!

Crime and Punishment

Let's start with a very tricky subject – crime and punishment. Almost every society in history has

drawn up a list of things it thinks are wrong, and for which people can be punished. This list can be almost endless. In Britain there are hundreds of offences it's possible to commit – everything from murder and robbery to beeping your car horn after 11.30pm! In the past, there have been all sorts of weird and wonderful laws – things like Elizabeth I's law, which forced everyone to wear a flat cap on Sundays, or a sixteenth-century ban on football and bowls.

Every society needs laws to protect people from those who would harm them. If you were starting from scratch, can you think of at least ten offences for which people could be punished? Some of them, like murder and burglary, are obvious. Then there are the other offences that you can make up for yourself. I'd ban people from wearing personal stereos on trains and buses. I hate litter, so I'd certainly ban that. And I'd make cruelty to animals a crime. What crimes would you outlaw? If you come up with more than ten, write them on a separate sheet of paper and slip it into the back of the book.

IF I RULED THE WORLD, MY CRIME LIST WOULD INCLUDE:

1 _____

2 _____

3 _____

4 _____

5 _____

6 _____

7 _____

8 _____

9 _____

10 _____

It's all very well passing these laws, but what are you going to do if people don't obey them? In most societies lawbreakers are punished in some way. Some societies have very severe penalties. For example, in strongly Islamic countries the punishment for stealing is to have your hand cut off. In other countries, like Britain, people who steal are sent to prison or fined.

What are your feelings about punishment? Some people are very keen on the idea of bringing back hanging and the birch (a punishment in which the offender is caned with a stick) and long sentences to deal with criminals. Others prefer different measures, including making the offender do community work, like painting and gardening, in an attempt to teach him or her to understand why their behaviour is wrong. What do you think about the crime problem? How would you tackle it?

IF I RULED THE WORLD, MY CRIME POLICY

WOULD BE: _____

_____

_____

WORLD RULER

In the section below you will find descriptions of five crimes. Imagine that you are the judge. What sentences would you impose on each of the offenders?

MY PUNISHMENTS TO FIT THE CRIME:

1 A burglar breaks into your neighbours' house while they are away on holiday. He steals their television, stereo and other valuables. What

sentence would you pass on him? _____

_____

_____

2 A man has been caught travelling on a Tube train without a ticket. When he is caught, he tries to run away. The cost of the ticket would have been £1. What is your sentence? _____

_____

_____

3 An elderly lady has been mugged on her way to the shops. The mugger has knocked her on the head and stolen her handbag. She is quite badly hurt, and still in hospital. What sentence would you pass? _____

_____

_____

4 An armed robber walks into a bank and tells the cashier to hand over the money. When the cashier hesitates, the robber shoots and kills him. What punishment would you impose on the robber?

_____

_____

_____

5 Three boys all of them aged thirteen have vandalised the local library, smashing windows, spraying graffiti and tearing up books. What is your sentence on them? _____

_____

_____

War and Peace

It's a sad fact that there has hardly ever been a time when, somewhere in the world, one nation was not at war with another. It's just as bad today. You don't believe me? Open today's newspaper and I bet you that there will be news of at least one conflict – between Arabs and Israelis in Palestine, or the Iranians and Iraqis, or Russia and Afghanistan, or even close at home in Northern Ireland. In the past there have been many attempts to try to find a way of ending wars, but very few of them have worked. No two nations seem to think along exactly the same lines, and there's a recipe for trouble.

As ruler of the world, can you think of anything you could do to keep the peace? Perhaps you could start by getting representatives of all the different nations along to talk together. This is already being done by groups like the United Nations, which includes America, Russia, France, China, Britain and other countries. The UN, as it is known, aims to keep the peace in the west. It also has its own 'army', which it sends to conflicts in other parts of the world in an attempt to stop wars. Unfortunately, it is not always successful. Would you copy the UN example, and get the leaders of all the nations around a huge table to talk?

If that idea doesn't appeal to you, how about confiscating all the world's weapons? You'd have to have an army of your own to do so, of course. And you might find that everyone wanted to fight you, in order to keep their weapons! Perhaps you can come up with an even better solution to the problem. Maybe young people like you should be put in charge of the armies. Maybe you should abolish nations and religion, and all the other things that cause wars – although it is a lot easier on paper than it is in practice. What's your brilliant solution to the problem of war?

IF I RULED THE WORLD, MY RECIPE FOR

WORLD PEACE WOULD BE: _____

_____

_____

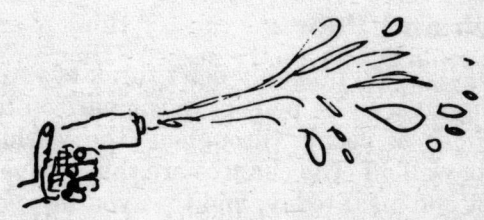

One of the great threats to the world today is the nuclear bomb. The very first atom bomb to be used in a war was dropped on the Japanese city of Hiroshima on 6 August 1945. The city was flattened and 136,000 people died. Forty years later, Russia and America have enough nuclear warheads to destroy the earth several times over. Many other countries also have their own nuclear weapons.

Some people worry about this, while others say that knowing that the west is so well armed makes them feel safer; they think that their enemies will be too frightened to attack. What do you feel about the idea of nuclear war? If you ruled the world, would you ban nuclear weapons? Would you build huge shelters so that people would be saved in the event of a war? Or don't you think that it will ever happen? Write your thoughts in the space below.

MY NUCLEAR POLICY: _____

_____

_____

Rich and Poor

Although you probably don't think of yourself as being a very rich person, in comparison to many millions of people throughout the world you're quite well off. The chances are that you've had at least one meal today, and that you have a house to live in and a bed to sleep in at night. Sorry to go on about such depressing things, but there are thousands of children who are not so lucky.

Does it ever bother you that some people are so very rich and others so very poor? If you ruled the world, would you choose to share the money around more evenly, or would you let things go on as they are at the moment?

MY POLICY ON WEALTH AND POVERTY: _

_____

_____

If you've chosen to share the money out more equally around the world, let's make a start on the problem of poverty by working out the basic needs of people around the world. Can you think of five things that everyone should have? For example, I think that if I ruled the world, I would do my best to make sure that everyone lived within a five-minute walk of a tap which had clean water. In Britain that sounds rather silly, but in parts of Africa and India people have to walk miles to find water. Taps would make life a lot easier. Can you come up with five other basic things of your own that everyone should have?

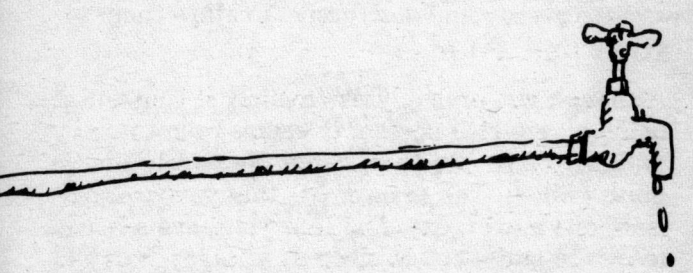

IF I RULED THE WORLD, THE FIVE BASICS FOR EVERYONE WOULD INCLUDE:

1 _____

2 _____

3 _____

4 _____

5 _____

Save the Whale and the Tiger

Not so long ago, Prince Charles made a speech pointing out that if we didn't take more care of our planet, within sixty years – during your lifetime – a third of all the lifeforms may be extinct. It may not seem very important now, but can you imagine having to describe to your grandchildren (because you will probably have grandchildren by then!) what a gorilla was like, or a tiger, because they're extinct? I've never met a whale or a dolphin while I've been swimming in the sea, but I'd hate to think of the world without them, simply because humans were too greedy and destructive to allow them to survive.

Of course, sometimes conservation can have unexpected results. For example, the Eskimo people of Canada used to make a living by slaughtering baby seals and selling the furs. A few years ago there was a terrible outcry about this, and the seal-culling, as it was known, was stopped. Now the Eskimos, who had been doing this for more than a hundred years, have lost their main source of income. They have no work and little money; their traditional way of life has come to an end.

How do you feel? If you ruled the world, would you care for the creatures — or does man matter more than the animals, as far as you're concerned?

IF I RULED THE WORLD, MY POLICY ON

WILDLIFE WOULD BE: _____

_____

_____

There are hundreds of endangered species around the world — everything from the panda to the white rhino. If you could choose to save one endangered animal from extinction, which would it be?

IF I RULED THE WORLD, THE ANIMAL I

WOULD SAVE WOULD BE: _____

_____

_____

WORLD RULER

Smoky Subject

Now for the subject that always gets people going – smoking. You probably know that the youngest age at which you are legally allowed to smoke is 16. And you probably also know several people at your school who started smoking when they were much younger than 16. Have you ever tried smoking? Go on, be honest. Do you want to be a smoker? If you do, I've got some news for you. You probably know it, but I'm going to say it anyway. Smoking is dangerous. It causes lung cancer and heart disease. What's more, it's not just the person

IS IT A HAIRSTYLE, IS IT A MAN WITH A SHEEP ON HIS HEAD, IS IT A TREE? NO, IT'S A . . . . !

who smokes who becomes ill. Recent studies have shown that people who live or work with smokers are also affected by smoke.

Despite this, millions of people around the world are smokers. In China, some children are encouraged to start to smoke very early, sometimes as young as three or four years of age. If you ruled the world, what would your policy on smoking be? There are a few practical facts to bear in mind. The first is the cost of looking after all the people who have made themselves (and others) ill by smoking. The second is that, the way things are run at the moment, cigarettes and tobacco raise a lot of money for the government because there is a tax imposed on each packet. So every time someone buys cigarettes, a few pence goes to the government. Naturally, the government doesn't want to lose this money, which is possibly why they're not very interested in banning smoking.

In some countries around the world, laws are coming into force banning smoking in public places. In America many companies ban smoking in offices. Do you think these are good ideas, or terrible ones? I know what I'd do about smoking.

I'd ban it altogether, and to make up for the lost tax, I'd make people pay to keep a dog or cat. If any smokers were unable to do without their cigarettes, I'd impose a very heavy tax on them to allow for the extra medical treatment they need. Does that sound too strict? What would your smoking policy be? You can put your opinion in the section below.

IF I RULED THE WORLD, MY SMOKING POLICY WOULD BE:

Would you ban smoking or not? _____

Because: _____

_____

_____

If you do ban smoking, what will you do for those

people who can't give up? _____

_____

_____

Answer these questions if you do not intend to ban smoking altogether:

If you didn't ban smoking, at what age would you

allow people to start? _____

_____

_____

Would you ban smoking in certain places? _____

_____

_____

Where? _____

_____

_____

What punishment would you have for people who

broke your law? _____

_____

_____

Cheers!

Now for something even more serious than smoking – alcohol. Smoking is a habit that usually only damages smokers themselves, but alcohol leads to thousands of innocent people being hurt in accidents and crime throughout the world. There's no doubt about it. If alcohol was a new discovery today, it would be considered so dangerous that it would be banned.

In America in 1920 there was an attempt to ban alcohol completely. It was called Prohibition, and anyone found in possession of alcohol was liable to fines and imprisonment. It didn't work. People brewed their own alcohol and gangsters like Al Capone made millions of dollars by smuggling booze into the country and selling it secretly. In 1933 Prohibition was scrapped. There are some countries, of course, where alcohol isn't allowed. These tend to be countries where religion prohibits alcohol. In Saudi Arabia, which is a Moslem country, alcohol is banned. People who are caught drinking it are punished very severely.

What are your thoughts about drink. Perhaps you think too much fuss is made about the dangers? In France, where they consume much more wine than the British do, lots of children are introduced to alcohol at an early age. If you've been abroad on holiday, you've probably noticed that the bars are open most of the day and that children are allowed to go into them. In Britain, the licensing laws have just been altered but children still can't go into pubs while their parents enjoy a drink. Is this sensible or would you like to see children drinking in pubs? Perhaps pubs should sell nothing but soft drinks? Fill in your opinions in the section below.

IF I RULED THE WORLD, MY POLICY ON ALCOHOL WOULD BE:

Would you ban alcohol or not? _____

Because: _____

_____

_____

If you do ban alcohol, how will you make sure that

it is not sold illegally? _____

_____

_____

If you would not ban alcohol, answer these questions.

Would you make any changes at all to the way alcohol is sold and pubs are run? _____

_____

_____

Because: _____

_____

_____

At what age would you allow people to drink in pubs? _____

_____

_____

Because _____

How would you punish a person who had drunk too much and (a) started a fight and (b) killed someone in a car crash? _____

_____

_____

Tax Time

I don't think I've ever met anyone who likes paying tax – but like it or not, if we didn't pay it our lives would be very difficult. Our tax pays for all kinds of things that we take for granted. It pays for our schools, for the police for the roads, for the National Health Service, for our libraries . . . in fact for every public service you can think of.

Looking back over the decisions you've taken in this book, you'll probably find that quite a few of them are expensive. Your amazing new palace will cost a million pounds or so, and if you've set up your own army to keep the peace around the world, that will cost millions more. Perhaps you've pledged to help the poor around the world – a very generous idea, but expensive. Or perhaps you're going to supply every child in the country with a free school uniform and free school meals. Terrific, but where is the money coming from?

The best way to raise money I think is by tax. There have been taxes on all sorts of things in the past, including windows and beards (no, I'm not joking!). Can you think of five things to tax to raise money for your world plans! I'd tax chocolate. Everyone eats it but it's not good for you, so if the tax stopped people eating it, it would be a good thing. And I'd tax ball-point pens. That would raise a lot of money, because everyone's always losing them! And, just to be silly, I'd tax people who eat crisps in the theatre. If you ruled the world, which three things would you tax?

IF I RULED THE WORLD, I'D TAX:

1 _____

2 _____

3 _____

And Finally . . .

What three laws would you pass to make the world a happier place? I'd make sure that everyone had a free holiday every year, so that they had a chance to get away from their problems. For my second law, I'd allow everyone to have two birthdays a year. And because no one likes getting old, I'd pass a third law so that people who had reached the age of forty could start counting their age backwards – so after they had reached forty, they would be thirty-nine the next year, and so on. I think that would make the world a bit happier, don't you? What would your three laws be?

MY THREE LAWS FOR A HAPPIER WORLD WOULD BE:

1 _____

2 _____

3 _____

Well, that's it. This book now contains a complete record of how you would rule the world if you had the chance — and a very good job you'd make of it! Of course, it's very unlikely that you will ever find yourself in charge of the whole world. But one day, when you're an adult, you may well find yourself running a small part of it — a family, or a school, or a business, or even, if you become Prime Minister, a country. Keep this book, and have a

look at it then. You may be surprised at how your ideas have changed.

One last thing. Every single one of us can play our part in making the world a better place. I'm going to start trying to improve it now – and I hope you will too.

BEAVER BESTSELLERS

You'll find books for everyone to enjoy from Beaver's bestselling range—there are hilarious joke books, gripping reads, wonderful stories, exciting poems and fun activity books. They are available in bookshops or they can be ordered directly from us. Just complete the form below and send the right amount of money and the books will be sent to you at home.

☐ THE ADVENTURES OF KING ROLLO	David McKee	£2.50
☐ MR PINK-WHISTLE STORIES	Enid Blyton	£1.95
☐ FOLK OF THE FARAWAY TREE	Enid Blyton	£1.99
☐ REDWALL	Brian Jacques	£2.95
☐ STRANGERS IN THE HOUSE	Joan Lingard	£1.95
☐ THE RAM OF SWEETRIVER	Colin Dann	£2.50
☐ BAD BOYES	Jim and Duncan Eldridge	£1.95
☐ ANIMAL VERSE	Raymond Wilson	£1.99
☐ A JUMBLE OF JUNGLY JOKES	John Hegarty	£1.50
☐ THE RETURN OF THE ELEPHANT JOKE BOOK	Katie Wales	£1.50
☐ THE REVENGE OF THE BRAIN SHARPENERS	Philip Curtis	£1.50
☐ THE RUNAWAYS	Ruth Thomas	£1.99
☐ EAST OF MIDNIGHT	Tanith Lee	£1.99
☐ THE BARLEY SUGAR GHOST	Hazel Townson	£1.50
☐ CRAZY COOKING	Juliet Bawden	£2.25

If you would like to order books, please send this form, and the money due to:
ARROW BOOKS, BOOKSERVICE BY POST, PO BOX 29, DOUGLAS, ISLE OF MAN, BRITISH ISLES. Please enclose a cheque or postal order made out to Arrow Books Ltd for the amount due including 22p per book for postage and packing both for orders within the UK and for overseas orders.

NAME ....

ADDRESS ....

....
Please print clearly.

Whilst every effort is made to keep prices low it is sometimes necessary to increase cover prices at short notice. Arrow Books reserve the right to show new retail prices on covers which may differ from those previously advertised in the text or elsewhere.

ACTIVITY BOOKS

If you enjoy making and doing fun things, perhaps you ought to try some of our exciting activity books. They are available in bookshops or they can be ordered directly from us. Just complete the form below and enclose the right amount of money and the books will be sent to you at home.

☐	THINGS TO MAKE IN THE HOLIDAYS	Steve and Megumi Biddle	£1.99
☐	CRAZY COOKING	Juliet Bawden	£2.25
☐	CRAZY PUPPETS	Delphine Evans	£1.95
☐	THINGS TO MAKE FOR CHRISTMAS	Eric Kenneway	£1.95
☐	THE PAPER JUNGLE	Satoshi Kitamura	£2.75
☐	SPRING CLEAN YOUR PLANET	Ralph Levinson	£1.75
☐	HOW TO MAKE SQUARE EGGS	Paul Temple and Ralph Levinson	£1.50
☐	COACHING TIPS FROM THE STARS: SOCCER	David Scott	£1.99
☐	FREAKY FASHIONS	Caroline Archer	£1.95

If you would like to order books, please send this form, and the money due to:
ARROW BOOKS, BOOKSERVICE BY POST, PO BOX 29, DOUGLAS, ISLE OF MAN, BRITISH ISLES. Please enclose a cheque or postal order made out to Arrow Books Ltd for the amount due including 22p per book for postage and packing both for orders within the UK and for overseas orders.

NAME ....

ADDRESS ....

....

Please print clearly.

Whilst every effort is made to keep prices low it is sometimes necessary to increase cover prices at short notice. Arrow Books reserve the right to show new retail prices on covers which may differ from those previously advertised in the text or elsewhere.

JOKE BOOKS

Have you heard about all the hilarious joke books published by Beaver? They are available in bookshops or they can be ordered directly from us. Just complete the form below and enclose the right amount of money and the books will be sent to you at home.

☐ THE SMELLY SOCKS JOKE BOOK	Susan Abbott	£1.95
☐ THE VAMPIRE JOKE BOOK	Peter Eldin	£1.50
☐ THE WOBBLY JELLY JOKE BOOK	Jim Eldridge	£1.50
☐ A JUMBLE OF JUNGLY JOKES	John Hegarty	£1.50
☐ NOT THE ELEPHANT JOKE BOOK	John Hegarty	£1.50
☐ THE CRAZY CRAZY JOKE BAG	Janet Rogers	£1.95
☐ THE CRAZIEST JOKE BOOK EVER	Janet Rogers	£1.50
☐ THE ELEPHANT JOKE BOOK	Katie Wales	£1.00
☐ THE RETURN OF THE ELEPHANT JOKE BOOK	Katie Wales	£1.50
☐ JOKES FROM OUTER SPACE	Katie Wales	£1.25
☐ SANTA'S CHRISTMAS JOKE BOOK	Katie Wales	£1.50

If you would like to order books, please send this form, and the money due to:
ARROW BOOKS, BOOKSERVICE BY POST, PO BOX 29, DOUGLAS, ISLE OF MAN, BRITISH ISLES. Please enclose a cheque or postal order made out to Arrow Books Ltd for the amount due including 22p per book for postage and packing both for orders within the UK and for overseas orders.

NAME ....

ADDRESS ....

....

Please print clearly.

Whilst every effort is made to keep prices low it is sometimes necessary to increase cover prices at short notice. Arrow Books reserve the right to show new retail prices on covers which may differ from those previously advertised in the text or elsewhere.